JOHN BU

by

R.D. Kernohan

Contents

Handsel 'Nutshell' Booklet no. 7

All rights reserved. No part of this publication may be reproduced, stored in a retrieval system, or transmitted in any form by any means, electronic, mechanical, photocopying, recording or otherwise, without the prior permission of The Handsel Press Ltd

British Library Cataloguing in Publication Data:
A catalogue record for this publication
is available from the British Library

ISBN   1 871828 55 4

© The Handsel Press 2000

Typeset in 10.5 pt. Garamond

Printed by Polestar Scientifica AUP, Aberdeen

Thanks are expressed to the Drummond Trust of 3 Pitt Terrace, Stirling, for assistance with the publication of this book

1 MAN OF MANY PARTS

John Buchan (1875-1940) is best known as writer of the adventure stories he called 'shockers'. Some of these, notably *The Thirty-nine Steps* and *Greenmantle*, are unsurpassable of their kind. They are minor literary masterpieces. A few of his novels, such as *Witch Wood*, also earn him a place in the serious literature of Scotland.

But Buchan was also a major writer of biography, history, and criticism, as well as a politician of some substance whose career took him to the House of Commons and then (as Lord Tweedsmuir) to be Governor-General of Canada.

He was, however, more significant even in his own time as a thinker and practical political philosopher than as an aspirant for office. He was also (like his distant kinsman on his mother's side, W.E. Gladstone) a considerable lay theologian, some of whose thinking about the Christian Faith and the Church under the pressures of the inter-war years will recover its relevance amid the different adversities of a new century.

Even before the Second World War he thought of Christianity as a minority faith in Europe and was convinced that the civilisation which expressed Christian values was no more than a veneer unless it rested on Christian religion. 'The Faith is being attacked and the attack is succeeding.' In this he reacted against such vanished idolatries as Communism, Nazism, Fascism, and the secularism of H.G. Wells or Bernard Shaw; but his attempt to reconcile Christian faith and liberal values, yet with a conservative view of institutions and society, retains its relevance. He quoted Blake's view that if the religion of Jesus is renounced man's natural need for religion will create a 'synagogue of satan'. The difference between his day and ours may be that such synagogues are no longer visible pseudo-Churches worshipping a Hitler or a trinity of Marx-Lenin-Stalin but tyrannies of secular assumptions and perverted liberal values.

Buchan's view of the world reflected his Christian inheritance of an evangelical strain of Scots Presbyterianism, the cultural shock of the First World War in which he lost a brother and close friends, and his easy passage via Oxford and marriage into a London 'Establishment' whose horizons were still imperial rather than parochial. But unlike many Scots lads o' pairts he was incorporated rather than assimilated. His literary and cultural interests, as well as his Reformed theology and Presbyterian eldership, reflected not only Scottish origins but a sense of Scottish identity.

That too has relevance today. Scottish identity, in a wider sense, is being expressed in new institutions and reflected in continuing debate about different

1

traditions in Scotland and different views about its relations with the rest of Britain and Europe. Buchan had important theological, literary, and political insights into Scottish identity - not least because he felt some of the tensions and even contradictions of Scottish life and history.

He had been raised in a manse which contrived to hold both Covenanting and Jacobite traditions in romantic affection. He was a broad-minded Tory who knew the hold of Liberal traditions for much of Scotland and the appeal of Socialist aspirations for other parts. See, for example, *Mr Standfast*, written several years before the Red Clydesiders came to Westminster. Two of his finest books were about great Scotsmen (both heroes to him) who expressed Scottish identity in very distinctive ways. One was Montrose, the 'Presbyterian Cavalier' - an elder and Covenanter who changed sides at a crisis. The other was Sir Walter Scott, another elder who inclined towards Episcopacy and, more significantly, used his literary powers to create a Scotland of romantic image and illusion and his political influence to resist not only revolution but reform.

From Buchan's own tensions and contradictions came some of his best literary work, too fashionable and highly praised in its day for his own good but of lasting value and as important in settling his place in Scottish and British cultural history as the 'shockers' which kept his name familiar in the decades after his death.

In addition to the biographies of Scott and Montrose this core of very diverse achievement includes the marvellous assessment of the Scots language (and of Burns) in the introduction to his Scots anthology, *The Northern Muse*. This is a definitive assessment of the situation just as Hugh MacDiarmid was emerging. MacDiarmid appears in the anthology, with one poem, as C.M. Grieve. This significant core of Buchan's work also includes the book which in which he and Sir George Adam Smith celebrated and commemorated the reunion of Scots Presbyterianism in 1929.

Much that Buchan wrote was enjoyable but trivial. Much that he said and wrote in more serious vein was necessarily ephemeral. But there remains much of value, not only in his 'serious' writing but in the adventure stories, which become all the more enjoyable when read with a knowledge of Buchan's views on Scots speech, British politics, history, and religion. Read in that way, some of them also include important elements of allegory and reflections on human condition and divine command.

In recent years interest in Buchan has revived, and those who had continued to read and enjoy his books, who always included many who differed from him in politics or religion or both, need no longer worry about being out of fashion, for what that matters. Some books have stayed in print. Others have come back into print. Andrew Lownie has added another notable biography to the 1965 one by Janet Adam Smith. He has also edited collections of Buchan's short stories and poetry. Buchan has been recognised too as as a serious and balanced military historian of the First World War, given the perspectives and sources available at the time. His respect and support for another Brasenose Presbyterian, Douglas Haig, remains controversial, but it is shared by a substantial body of historians and no longer to be dismissed as either sycophantic or ill-informed.

Buchan has been recognised, as Kipling has been, as a writer and thinker whose significance survives the later twentieth century's changes not only in political power but in values and shibboleths. Even a slighting and hostile reference, such as Christopher Harvie's claim that Kipling was 'politically a much nastier animal than Buchan' unwittingly draws attention to the way in which literary work outlasts the political and social conditions from which it emerged and which it reflected.

Buchan has also been acquitted, certainly by those who have properly read the evidence, of the 1960's assumption that he was a reactionary imperialist racist with a tinge of anti-semitism. The evidence is well presented by his biographers Janet Adam Smith and Andrew Lownie, and he emerges as a Christian friend of Judaism, and a supporter of imperial evolution into Commonwealth.

He was, in fact, a moderate supporter of Zionism and of Jewish identity, coming as he did from a strain of evangelical Presbyterianism much concerned with Jewish return to the Land of Israel and hoping that the people of Israel would be both a nation and a national Church of the Messiah. He was also a severe critic of Hitler's persecution of the Jews. The John Buchan Centre at Broughton displays the certificate of his enrolment in the Jewish National Fund's 'golden book'.

Buchan also recognised better than most of his imperialist contemporaries, including his old master, Lord Milner, that the future of South Africa depended first on reconciliation of Britons and Boers and, in the very much longer run, on African advancement. His own words, deeds, and thoughts vindicate him and settle the way character and dialogue should be interpreted, whether in the Hannay novels or *Prester John*. Richard Hannay is not Buchan, though he sometimes speaks for Buchan. The same is true for David Crawfurd, the Scot who gets on in South Africa, and Sir Edward Leithen, the successful barrister-politician. But minor characters who, in character, make anti-semitic comments, like Scudder in *The Thirty-nine Steps*, do not speak for Buchan at all. The author's known and explicitly declared views - whether on Zionism, Africa, Scotland, or the Christian faith - are a guide to when he may agree with his characters.

There is no doubt that Buchan is back to stay as a significant figure in Scottish cultural history and English literature. However, there is both an opportunity and a need to emphasise the missing dimension in this rehabilitation: Buchan's Christian faith and his belief that 'civilisation must have a Christian basis and must ultimately rest on the Christian Church'. That dimension is insufficiently emphasised even in some of the very good writing about Buchan which has appeared in recent years. It is important for a true understanding of the man and his books as well as of his concepts of British history, Western civilisation, and Scottish identity.

This brief study of Buchan tries to analyse different aspects of the achievement of this man of many parts, startling versatility, and exceptional capacity of mind and for work. 'He could move on a score of stages in a score of infinitely various parts with equal ease and equal dignity', said the famous London minister, Dr Archibald Fleming. For all his work-load he always seemed to have time to spare, and he could listen as readily as speak. But Buchan was not an actor; the many parts and very different achievements were parts of himself. That is why it is important to recognise the quality of the popular novelist as well as of the biographer and historian whose personal life and and view of civilisation were both deeply affected by the First World War. That ordeal shaped much of what he did and thought both as a practical politician and as a political philosopher who was also a lay theologian. Finally, Buchan deserves study both an an interpreter of Scottish identity and culture and as an example of the personal complexities of belief, inheritance, tastes, and experience which help to create that identity.

These reflections on his creative work and opinions are inevitably closely related to ambitions and incidents in his personal life and career. It is sensible, as a prelude to them, to summarise who he was and what he did.

John Buchan was born in 1875 in Perth where his father, son of a Peebles lawyer, was a Free Church of Scotland minister. He belonged to that mainstream of the Disruption tradition which in 1900 merged with the heirs of various secessions to form the United Free Church and in 1929 reunited with the 'Establishment'. John was the first-born of four brothers and two sisters. The next child was Anna, who was to succeed as a popular novelist under the pseudonym of O. Douglas.

Their mother was Helen Masterton, daughter of a Broughton sheep-farmer and on her mother's side a kinswoman of the greatest Victorian Liberal, William Ewart Gladstone. Buchan grew up in manses in Fife and Glasgow, though some of the most formative childhood influences on him were those of upper Tweeddale, where he spent childhood summers on the Masterton farm. In Glasgow he went to Hutchesons' Grammar School (then in the Gorbals, near his father's church) and in 1892, aged 17, to the university across the river at Gilmorehill, where one of the influences on him was the young professor of Greek, Gilbert Murray. He carried on to Brasenose College, Oxford and took a First in Greats in 1899. He was also president of the Union and a notable university prize-winner but missed a fellowship of All Souls. Though called to the English Bar, he had already been making a living by writing and as a publisher's adviser before going to South Africa in the final stages of the Boer War as assistant private secretary to the High Commissioner and pro-consul, Lord Milner. He returned to law and writing in London in 1903, adding a legal work on the taxation of foreign income to his growing list of books and articles. He also returned not only to familiar Border and Galloway hills but to mountaineering in Scotland and Europe. His slight build and at times indifferent health went with great physical as well as mental determination.

In 1906 his literary aptitudes and his Oxford friendship with Thomas Nelson, of the Scottish publishing family, led to an appointment as adviser on books and partner in the firm. In 1907 he married Susan Grosvenor, acquiring the 'perfect comrade' and a 'vast new relationship - Grosvenors, Wellesleys, Stuart-Wortleys, Lytteltons, Talbots'. They had three sons and a daughter; Susan Tweedsmuir survived him by 37 years. In 1912 he became an elder in the Scots congregation of St Columba's Pont Street, situated then as now round the back of Harrods but in the original building destroyed in a 1941 air raid. In the same year he was shaken by the death of his brother William, who had also gone to Brasenose and was rising rapidly in the Indian Civil Service.

During the First World War he became a war correspondent and later an Intelligence Corps major working in what would now be called Haig's public relations for the headquarters of the British Expedionary Force in France. He moved to be a 'director' in the Ministry of Information, ranking as a lieutenant-colonel. (Hence the frequent post-war references to 'Colonel Buchan'.) He also found time to develop the 'Richard Hannay' novels, starting with *The Thirty-nine Steps*, which was completed in 1914 when its author was under doctor's orders to rest.

After the war, in which his youngest brother Alastair, Thomas Nelson, and many friends had been killed, Buchan wrote in a more definitive form the war history which had begun as a near-contemporary narrative for Nelson's, originally published in parts. He also developed his interest in Tory politics, first evident as prospective Unionist candidate after 1911 in the Liberal but near-marginal county constituency of Peebles and Selkirk, awaiting a General Election aborted by war. However, the Irish Home Rule crisis and other political tensions of the time had created something like the atmosphere of a permanent election campaign. Eventually he became Conservative M.P. for the Scottish Universities (1927-35), though he had made his home from 1920 at Elsfield, near Oxford. He continued to write popular novels and 'romances' but devoted more time to biographies, including those of Cromwell, Scott, and Montrose - the last a successful new version of a pre-war work which had been severely criticised by historians.

He was talked of as a possible Cabinet Minister. As his latest biographer, Andrew Lownie, has shown, he would have been more responsive to a major political offer than his own memoirs might suggest. Before going to Canada he was approached about a possible governorship of Burma, then about to be hived off from India, and hoped he might revive an old love by becoming Governor-General of South Africa. In 1933 and 1934 he was Lord High Commissioner (i.e. representative of the Crown) to the General Assembly of the Church of Scotland and in 1935-40, Governor-General of Canada, where he wrote a life of the Roman Emperor Augustus and died in 1940 aged 64. He had been made Lord Tweedsmuir of Elsfield in 1935. For the last two years of his life he had been chancellor of Edinburgh University. He also remained till his death an elder at St Columba's Pont Street. He left two major works to be published posthumously - the valedictory Canadian novel *Sick Heart River*, in which Edward Leithen finds grace goes with good works, and an autobiography, *Memory Hold-the-Door*.

Despite the fulfilment he found in Canada, it was as a writer that Buchan was to be best remembered: a writer who was a thinker and scholar as well as an entertainer.

2 MASTER OF THE 'SHOCKER'

Buchan was more than 200 pages into his autobiography before he had something to say, and then not all that much, about the literary genre for he which he is most widely remembered and which he indisputably mastered: the thriller, or as he called it when delivering *The Thirty-nine Steps* for publication, the 'shocker'.

Even in the retrospect of fame and success he was rather cursory, slightly apologetic, and even dismissive. The books had a wide sale, he confessed, 'and I always felt a little ashamed that profit should accrue from what had given me so much amusement.' Even the creation of his most popular hero, Richard Hannay, was excused as the result of being pinned to his bed in the early months of the war and 'compelled to keep my mind off too tragic realities'.

It is arguable whether this well-controlled flutter of conscience owes most to the inheritance of Calvinism or of classicism, or even to his mother's literary preferences. She, it seems, was mildly shocked by the vigour of language and action. But Buchan had a proper sense of both duty and calling, allied to a range of talents, supply of energy, and increasing stores of erudition and experience. He also had an entrance pass to what would later be called the corridors of power. He could not find fulfilment in the adventures of Richard Hannay or Dickson McCunn any more than Conan Doyle could in the dazzling success of Sherlock Holmes. Doyle tried but spectacularly failed to dispose of Holmes in the Reichenbach Falls. Buchan dealt with Hannay after the war by sending him to Parliament and allowing him only two more narrative novels and occasional mentions elsewhere, plus a few bits and pieces like the prologue to *The Courts of the Morning*.

Those who know Buchan only from a few popular books or by reputation will be tempted to think he allowed himself to be diverted from what he was best at by what he wanted to be, and that posterity was the loser. They are mistaken, for Buchan was as good a writer in other fields which he was entitled to regard as more important, and also a significant thinker. It was his political ambitions, always less clearly defined and pursued, which were only partly fulfilled, not his literary ones. But it would also be a mistake to distort Buchan's own mildly deprecatory view of his adventure stories into a definitive judgment on him or them. You do no honour to the biographer of Scott and Montrose by trivialising the achievement in *Greenmantle* or refusing to suspend disbelief, enjoy improbability, and share the excitement of the pursuit in *The Thirty-nine Steps*.

The adventure stories and romances - Buchan distinguished between them - are good of their kind; and the best of them superb. They display the power of narrative, the pace of plot, the turn of phrase, the ear for dialogue (not least the Scots dialogue) and often a vigorous and vivid power of characterisation appropriate for the genre. In *Greenmantle* for example part of the success comes not from the Danubian travelogue and the imaginative (and propagandist) sense of life far beyond the enemy lines but from the success of Richard Hannay's supporting cast: the dyspeptic Blenkiron, the far-fetched Sandy Arbuthnot, and even the Boer hunter Peter Pienaar, who has a freshness and credibility which he largely lost when allowed to take to the air and reappear in *Mr Standfast*.

But it is with Hannay himself that Buchan, perhaps unconsciously, demonstrated the quality of his art and his contribution to the thriller as an art-form. Much effort has been spent in linking Hannay to particular individuals, notably the professional soldier Lord Ironside; and certainly, like lesser characters, Hannay has traits or experiences of people that Buchan knew. But caution is needed, not only because Buchan's heroes are imaginative composites but because they may reflect different influences in different books. For the example the critic T.J. Binyon argues persuasively in his introduction to the Everyman edition of *The Courts of the Morning* that, although the Sandy Arbuthnot of *Greenmantle* may have been modelled on Aubrey Herbert, he had been remodelled on T.E. Lawrence to become the hero of *The Courts of the Morning*. The argument is persuasive, even for Hannay devotees who cannot accept Binyon's other argument, that Sandy got the role because the safe, solid Hannay could not be cast as a guerrilla leader in South America.

In some things Hannay is improbably lucky and improbably gifted - for example in his command not only of mining engineering but of fluent German, Afrikaans, Sesutu, American and Australian English, and various shades of Scots. He also has a startling rise in rank over the wartime books from temporary captain to major-general, though it should be noted in extenuation that Buchan's hero in another sense, Haig, though so often portrayed as a dim and devious cavalryman, made an Australian Jewish engineer militia officer, John Monash, into one of his best corps commanders.

More important, Buchan used Hannay to create a narrator and at times a commentator detached from himself and yet with something of himself, for example a devotion to John Bunyan's *Pilgrim's Progress*. Hannay evolves from the plain-speaking and uncomplicated colonial engineer, out of sorts in London at the start of *The Thirty-nine Steps*, by way of *Greenmantle* and a 'good war', to the war-wearied, reflective, but still determined and soon to be married hero of *Mr Standfast*. And by then something should be apparent that becomes more explicit in the later Hannay novels: that the thrillers which can be enjoyed at a simpler level contain important elements of allegory.

Significantly, the most important of the Hannay novels, though not the best in the literary sense, is *Mr Standfast*, which takes its title and part of its theme from John Bunyan's greatest of English allegories. The battle of good and evil is more than a conventional framework for a thriller. That remains true for *The Three Hostages* and *The Island of Sheep*, even when the the powers of darkness no longer have the neat, covenient shape dicated both by the exigencies of war and by Buchan's conviction that that British and Allied cause was a just one. The novels also express, for those who want more than a lively tale, the fragility of civilisation and the pervasive power of evil. Buchan professed never to have been in fear of the Devil; but something diabolical seems to possess some of his characters, by no means all stock villains. The theme is developed in a more complex way in his serious romance of the inter-war years, *Witch Wood*, a seventeenth-century tale set around Broughton in the 'Tweedside parish of my youth'. But then the powers of evil are not using Germans or even rogue politicians but a delinquent elder.

The essential seriousness of even the 'shockers' is well summarised in Donald Smith's brief entry on Buchan in the notable *Dictionary of Scottish Church History and Theology* (1993): 'His books are often popular in form but evoke serious concerns, particularly the conflict with evil and the regeneration of the self, both strongly Calvinist themes.'

Another factor which often separates the classic thriller from pulp fiction and elevates it to a place in literature is the ability of an author to add to the skills of narrative and the sustenance of excitement an ability to create an atmosphere and express a mood, especially of a time and place. What commands a minor place in literary history may then become a significant part of social history. Holmes and Watson are an expression of Victorian values and part of British history, not just a legend of Baker Street as it never really was. Raymond Chandler could labour his plots but his Philip Marlowe deploys a narrative gift and turn of phrase - often imitated, never matched - that go with a sense of atmoshere. From these colours came an impressionist's picture of Los Angeles as it may just possibly once have been. Eric Ambler's talents and Ian Fleming's successes with James Bond, for all his limitations and excesses, merit a place on a less eminent shelf of the same library.

In recent years Frederick Forsyth and John Le Carré have probably squeezed in beside them. Jeffrey Archer may even be allowed a passing mention, if only because he has claimed that Richard Hannay is his favourite hero. Even Dickens, in *A Tale of Two Cities*, wandered away from the novel of social purpose and constructive caricature into the adventure story on a grand scale and against a conventionally-painted but wonderfully vivid backdrop of the French Revolution.

Buchan also shared with Chandler what some determined thriller-writers conspicuously lack: an occasional and never unkind sense of humour. Richard Hannay is frustrated in seeking news of Portland Place murder hunt in *The Scotsman*. 'I could find very little about anything except a thing called the General Assembly - some ecclesiastical spree, I gathered.' He also raises a cheer, in one of his many disguises, by telling a Liberal meeting, chaired by a weaselly minister with a red nose, that 'there were no Tories in Australia, only Labour and Liberals'.

Perhaps Buchan's insistence on not taking the 'shockers' too seriously at the time is one of the reasons why the best of them were good enough to survive and, within their limitations, to be taken seriously long after being written. They inevitably reflect not only Buchan's own values and assumptions but the styles and fashions of the various sets to which he belonged or with whom he mixed. They also probably reflect the banalities of upper-class conversation as faithfully as they do the cadences of the Scots vernacular speech

Buchan knew best. Note, for example, that in *Mr Standfast* he contrives, to the benefit of the dialogue, to have Hannay introduced to the Red Clyde by a Border radical and plants an exiled postmistress from Annandale in Morvern. The books were hurriedly written, but with art, care, and precision. They depend on pace and plot, but also on the quality and character Buchan brought to the narrative - something not only hard to imitate in print but difficult to adapt for another medium. Alfred Hitchcock's film version of *The Thirty-nine Steps* is famous but it is not Buchan and such a distortion as to be almost a travesty. None of the other TV and film adaptations of Buchan books is really memorable. Radio, however, is another matter, for it depends so much on power, style, and character in narration, and on the authentic ring of dialogue - Buchan's greatest assets. He was, as his eldest son said in the first issue of *The John Buchan Journal*, 'a natural writer of romance whose plots came almost unbidden to him'.

His adventure stories and romances are worth reading both for their own sake and as reflections of many of the ideas and convictions which influenced him as a biographer, political thinker, practical philsopher, and even theologian. He would be remembered for them if he had done nothing else; but he did much else. His biographies, as the second Lord Tweedsmuir said, 'were intensely personal creations. An historical character would suddenly fill him with an interest of such burning intensity that he was forced into writing his biography.'

That interest and that intensity, however, reflected even more than the themes of the thrillers and romances the deepest concerns of Buchan's life: the good life, the nature and fragility of civilisation, the interaction of tradition and reform, the relation of the State and the individual, and the nature, destiny, and chief end of man - defined in the Calvinist Shorter Catechism as 'to glorify God and enjoy him forever'.

3 WRITER AND THINKER

Buchan's view of the world was shaped by two major influences and one relatively minor one. It was later to be darkened and deepened by the First World War, both as a disaster for European civilisation and as the cause of much personal grief.

Both by belief and in background Buchan was a Christian, immersed in an inheritance of faith but also living in the Faith and seeking to relate it to the intellectual, moral, and practical problems of his time. That was the first and supreme influence.

The other great influence was that he was also the product of an intensely classical education, starting with Latin tuition from his father. He found his 'first real intellectual interest in the Latin and Greek classics' just before going to Glasgow University, but Hutchesons' Grammar School had equipped him to pursue it. At Glasgow his strongest subject was Latin but the youthful Professor Gilbert Murray, later to be a leading advocate of the League of Nations, broadened his interest in Greek and introduced him to Hellenism at a time when he was already exploring English, Scottish, and Continental philosophy. His Oxford First in Greats meant that he had mastered the 'dead' languages as a prelude to another almost total immersion, this time in the literature, history, and philosophy of the Greek and Roman civilisations from which Christian Europe emerged.

Buchan claimed that the fundamentals of Christian belief were so entwined with his nature that he neither questioned them nor found any need for philosophy to rationalise them, 'for they seemed to me completely rational'. He also claimed that, without ever consciously rejecting the idea of Christianity as a system of penalties and rewards - the 'cosmology of the elder Calvinism' which faded from his consciousness - his involvement with classical literature, history, and philosophy not only broadened and mellowed the Calvinism of his youth but confirmed it. As he encountered and interpreted them, they enjoined humility, simplicity, even austerity, and nourished a sense of the transience of life, the dignity and frailty of human nature, and need for the temporal to look to the eternal. They gave him a respect for the power of myth, in the deeper sense of the word, and may have influenced his sense of the supernatural, most evident in short stories. The classical civilisations defined the human condition, and posed the questions to which, as a Christian, he found the answers in Jesus Christ in whom the Word was made flesh and dwelt among us, full of grace and truth, as the Light of the World.

The third but relatively minor influence was his adherence to political Conservatism, a pragmatic and empirical creed which had survived into the twentieth century by absorbing a good deal of nineteenth-century Liberalism but which still offered a home for Tory romantics and Tory reformers. In Scotland especially, that survival owed much to the revolt of the Liberal Unionists against Gladstone's Irish policy, as well as a more gradual recoil of conservative Liberals in business and the professions from radical policies that might seem to lead not only to democracy but to socialism. A substantial part of the Scottish Liberal middle class, among them the Buchans, had moved towards the Conservatism which fought under the Unionist title, and which, when John Buchan nursed his Border constituency as a prospective candidate, was led by another son of the Presbyterian manse, Andrew Bonar Law, who was a seat-holder (but not a fellow-elder) at St Columba's Pont Street.

Almost a century later it is probably easier for many admirers of John Buchan's books, however spectacularly varied their own political opinions may be, to grasp the signficance of his political commitment and associations - subordinate though they were in his life - than to appreciate the power of the greater formative influences. Relatively few bright students of the early twenty-first century will easily recognise the fundamentals of Christian belief as both rational and 'entwined in his nature'. Even fewer will depend on the Latin and Greek classics for the main stimulus to their intellectual development.

In politics Buchan was a moderate, almost a 'trimmer' in the best sense of the term, though in politics, as in personal life and religious belief, he had a strong sense of authority: one lived under lawful authority and, according to one's station in life and family situation, one exercised it. Some Tories, making the mistake of assessing people out of their context of time and place, might label him (in the idiom of Margaret Thatcher's prime) as a 'Wet'. His politics certainly took account of human feelings and reactions much more than of abstract theories - for he would not have regarded respect for the institutions of family, Church, and constitutional monarchy as an abstract theory but as a reflection of the natural order of things. He was of a conservative cast of mind, quoting the moderate seventeeth-century Cavalier Lord Falkland: 'When it is not necessary to change it is necessary not to change.' But he was also, though explicitly rejecting Socialism, a believer in what he called 'the progressive socialisation of the State', by which he meant that public policy and institutions should reflect social concerns and intervene to meet social needs.

Indeed one of the not entirely resolvable problems about Buchan as historian and political thinker is to decide how far his literary involvement in the seventeenth century shaped his assessment of British politics, especially in the inter-war years, and how far his own political approach determined his historical judgments.

He professed enthusiasm for the ideal of 'the Presbyterian Cavalier' and cited three examples: the Virginian 'Stonewall' Jackson, who came to Presbyterianism through marriage; the notably taciturn Earl Haig, also of Brasenose and the Borders; and James Graham, the Marquis of Montrose, an elder who signed the National Covenant of 1638, led the armed Scottish protest against Charles I, but took the king's side after 1642, creating havoc for a time in Scotland when the Covenanting Government sent the main Scottish army to join in the English Civil War. They are an oddly-assorted trio and it was Montrose who mattered most for Buchan, both in terms of serious historical interest and in the bid to go beyond an apt phrase and all those battles long ago into an exploration of political theory.

Buchan's main treatment of this theme is in his 1928 biography of Montrose, a substantial contribution both to history and Scottish literature. It drew out much of the best in Buchan, not least because his pride had been hurt when an earlier version of the same subject (1913) had been severely criticised by such Church historians as David Hay Fleming and W.L. Mathieson. However some of his serious historical and political thinking also comes into his fiction. The realism which, as with Sir Walter Scott, tempered his Jacobite romanticism, is evident after a fashion and harnessed to creative imagination in one of the best of his earlier short-stories, *The Company of the Marjolaine* (1908). In the tale he imagines an American deputation in the aftermath of the War of Independence coming to Europe in search of a king. They reluctantly resign themselves to Republicanism after encountering Charles Edward Stuart as he was in his latter days of decline and drunkenness, forty years after the Forty-five. But realism is banished when Montrose appears, as a minor character with a big speech, in the dramatic novel *Witch Wood* (1927).

The setting for the exposition of the rule of law under the Crown is Scotland in the Civil Wars involving Charles I, the English Parliament, and Covenanting Scotland. Montrose appears disguised as a groom and enters into a political and theological dialogue with the sorely tried young Tweedside minister who is the book's ostensible hero. 'If you upset the just proportion of the law you will gain not liberty but confusion', argues this most articulate of grooms, a supporter of the National Covenant but not of the Solemn League and Covenant concluded with the English Parliamentarian party. The one is a Covenant of Grace the other a Covenant of Works in which the Kirk steps beyond its proper bounds and is weakened in its proper duties, comforting the afflicted and guiding souls to Heaven.

Montrose declares allegiances which are also Buchan's own in a later age. 'I am an orthodox son of the Kirk, a loyal subject of His Majesty, and a passionate Scot.' The State is a body which needs a just proportion among its members. The law may be changed by the people's will, but till changed it is to be revered and obeyed: a view certainly held by Buchan and possibly by Montrose but not quite worded as Charles I would have wanted: he went to the scaffold maintaining that sovereign and subject were 'clean different'.

Buchan, however, is not merely linking his historical interpretation of Montrose's principles, which led to excommunication as well as outlawry and execution, with an abstract political philosophy of his own which crops up in unexpected places, as when the successful South American revolutionaries in *The Courts of the Morning* apologise for adhering to the local custom of having

13

a Republic. It is not at all far-fetched to relate arguments in Buchan's writing on the seventeenth century to the different threats to civil peace and claims for revolutionary reforms - for a time there was none too clear a line between revolution and reform - which he himself knew from the turbulence on Clydeside at the end of the war, the Troubles in Ireland, and the General Strike of 1926, which seemed something like a bloodless civil war in Britain itself. It is also possible to argue that Buchan's approach may have relevance in many sorts and conditions of political quarrels quite different in their setting either from seventeenth-century religious and constitutional conflicts or from twentieth-century industrial ones. It is not a universal formula, not even a general theory, and it is unco hard to relate effectively to tyrannical governments, which is why the Scots Covenanters had a better case against Montrose than Buchan conceded, but it is a cast of mind and conscience applicable in differing degrees to different situations.

Is it also possible to relate some of Buchan's religious experience and insight into cultural and spiritual conditions of Scotland, Britain, and what was Christendom, even though they are very different both from those of his youth and those, recast by war and revolution, of his prime and his fame? That is more difficult, but far from impossible. It is also valuable if proper allowance is made for the vast social and intellectual changes since his time.

Take even that enormous, if insufficiently recognised, change in the relation of our culture to the classics. It is neither merely nor mainly, as is sometimes thought, a change from a literary culture to a scientific or technological one, but a drastic reshuffle of priorities, sources, values, and role-models within the whole area of literature, humane studies, morality, the social sciences, and (for those who even recognise a spiritual dimension) comparative religion.

Buchan would have had far less trouble with the heirs and successors of Einstein than with Reich, the latter-day disciples of Durkheim, or even Germaine Greer, though feminists should remember that Richard Hannay got his orders from Mary Lamington, even before he married her. Had Buchan been spared to reflect at length on the long-term influence of Freud and Freudians, he would probably have offered the kind of assessment that he made of Calvin, recognising the stature and quality of the man but looking askance at some of those who attached themselves to his name.

The remarkable thing is not that some of Buchan's thinking is inevitably dated. That is the standing threat to all theology and philosophy that strives for contemporary social and intellectual relevance. More remarkable is that a good deal of it is of enduring value.

Some of it was prophetic in its time. For example, in *The Company of the Marjolaine*, the aged Young Chevalier warns 'The world will ever have need of kings... those later kings created by the people will bear a harsher hand than the old race who ruled as of right'. The remarkable thing is that this was written in 1908, before Lenin, Stalin, Mussolini, Hitler, and the endless line of popular despots emerging from nationalism and the end of imperialism.

The same is true, perhaps more profoundly, of Buchan's thinking after the First World War, in which he had been a good public relations man, a superb propagandist, and as competent and fair a contemporary historian as the conditions of the time allowed. It may be true, as critics have suggested, that he was never at ease in the post-war world, with its rival dogmatisms, rejection of the past, and rapidly changing moods - brittle prosperity, deep depression, and preparation for renewed conflict. He shared with millions a sense of personal loss: in his case of his younger brother Alastair, killed at Arras in 1917 in the same battle as his friend and business partner, Thomas Nelson, and of many friends: 'the best of the Pilgrims', as Mary Lamington had warned Hannay in *Mr Standfast*.

It was not a world to be at ease in, but from Buchan's attempt to adjust to it came some of his best work. The lives of Montrose and Cromwell showed his understanding of two complex men who reacted very differently in simplifying their choice in a revolutionary crisis; and, because the regicide Cromwell demanded a greater effort of sympathy from Buchan (the Presbyterian Cavalier), that biography may be a greater work of art, if not of history, than the life of Montrose. If the Cromwell book has a weakness it is in sometimes allowing the fascination of the military history to overshadow the political and the personal. Even Buchan's life of the Roman Emperor Augustus (1937) was a conscious effort to relate themes from classical times to contemporary concepts of dictatorship and empire.

But the challenge of which Buchan was most conscious in the last phase of his life was the decline of the authority which mattered most to him: the authority of the Christian faith as the basis and inspiration both of the good life and of a culture and civilisation. With that went recognition of the authority of the Church, both as a visible institution and expression of the faith and as a concept of 'the whole number of the elect that have been, are, or shall be be gathered into one under Christ the head thereof'.

It is appropriate to quote that Calvinist definition of the Church from the Westminster Confession, which Buchan thought the 'one worthy fruit' of the dealings of the Covenanters with the English Puritans. He shared the Confession's theory of the relation of the Church to the civil power and even more its distinctively Calvinist view of the institutional Church, with three ideas blended in a way which marked off the main Reformed tradition from Anglicanism, Roman Catholicism, and nonconforming Protestantism. For he was a High Churchman in his view of the authoritative nature of the Church, a true heir of Melville and Chalmers in his insistence on the independence of the Church, and a Reformer in his acceptance of the fallibility of the institutions which express the human face of the divinely-instituted society. Buchan's work is often sympathetic to Anglican and Roman Catholic devotion - even Richard Hannay managed a kind allusion to Saint Teresa - and his last novel, *Sick Heart River*, was meant, among other things, to be complimentary to French-Canadian traditions. But although the narrative of Sir Edward Leithen's last days is given to a Roman priest, the account of a good life and death has a very Protestant ring, albeit with a stoic strain that hints at the classicism that accompanied Buchan's Christianity. Good works express the Christian life but salvation is by grace, and there is need neither for last sacrament nor for any mediator but Christ.

Theologically Buchan was a conservative liberal, though in applying his theology to social, political, and cultural concerns he was a liberal conservative. That is not a fashionable position today, even in the Scottish Church, but it is one which expresses the Christian conviction and political inclinations of many people in every Western Christian Communion. It is one which will always need to be to articulated while the Church remains an institution as well as a community - and surely it must be both - and related to a culture with Christian roots and permeated by Christian values. But he also saw himself as an evangelical, standing aloof from the Moderate and 'Enlightenment' traditions in Scots Presbyterianism because he found them lacking in warmth and enthusiasm, compared to Wesley in England and the 'supreme religious genius of Scotland', Thomas Chalmers. 'Conversion in its plain evangelical sense is still the greatest fact in any life', he wrote.

These views are scattered though Buchan's writing, sometimes argued, sometimes implied. They are most succinctly stated in an address to the 1937 conference of the World Presbyterian Alliance in Montreal. 'Theology is not a static thing and antiquarian accretions are no part of its essence. It is an attempt to systematise the divine revelation and to bring it into accord with every aspect of life.' But his approach is most elegantly set out in the book which Buchan wrote, in partnership with Sir George Adam Smith, to mark the reunion of almost all Scots Presbyterianism in 1929.

It is a brilliant contribution to Scottish and Reformed historical theology, even though some of Buchan's skills as politician, publicist, and propagandist are deployed to help every strand of Scots Presbyterianism feel at home in the reunited Church, not only spiritually at ease but historically vindicated.

Buchan's contribution was in effect a short history of the Reformed Church in Scotland, supplemented by an essay on the prospect for the reunited Church.

This set it, as part of the universal Church, in a far less triumphalist context than that of the 1929 reunion, an event whose importance to the Scotland of its day is hard for modern Scotland to appreciate: the part that still adheres to the Kirk takes its structural unity for granted; the rest of Scotland knows nothing and cares not at all.

Much of Buchan's 1929 analysis of the future is still valid, not least his reflections on a moral anarchism related to 'half-understood philosophic doctrines about the right of each man to self-realisation and the development of the personality'. He sought the discipline of a broad, rational and humane morality, 'the teaching of Christ', and recognised that fidelity to conventions was no basis for virtue.

'But', he wrote, 'disintegration is not a mood in which the world can long abide.' The last decade of his life was to be overshadowed by the consequences not only of the disintegration of Christendom but of the rival bids for a totalitarian, secular, and anti-Christian kind of reintegration. It was a situation in which Buchan returned to his old theme of the vulnerability of civilisation but with a new sense of the Faith being under attack. The attack was succeeding. Nominal Christians had grown cold in their devotion at a time when the quality of faith was being put to the test. 'In Europe, as in the era before Constantine, Christianity is in a minority.'

As the Second World War began his thoughts reverted to his feelings at stages in the earlier war that 'the stable universe was dissolving about us'. In his memoirs he professed to feel an undercurrent of optimism but he was more convincing in the way faith asserted itself amid the temporal uncertainties in which 'we are compelled to fumble... for the mist is too thick to see far down the road.' Dogmatism, he said, gives way to questioning, and questioning in the end to prayer.

He was dead before the first uncertain winter of the war was over. An accident hastened his death but even on his last visit to Britain, when *Sick Heart River* must have been taking shape in his mind, Archibald Fleming had thought him 'shrunken to a shadow' and a dying man. The obituaries were fulsome but his influence declined, except through the enjoyment of his books. It is probably easier now to supplement that enjoyment with a fair and profitable assessment of the author than it was in the decades after his death, with their new ordeals, and new illusions.

4 SCOTTISH IDENTITY

All identity is a blend of inheritance and experience. What we are is conditioned both by what we are told we are or taught to be, even if we react against it, and what we discover ourselves to have become. It reflects times past as well as contemporary assumptions; and that is true both of personal and national identity. We are creations of history and creatures of our times.

It is easy to present both Buchan's personality and his Scottishness in such terms. He was a son of a Free Kirk manse, and therefore an heir of the Evangelical tradition in Scottish Presbyterianism rather than the Moderate one. The latter was closer to his own philosophical and temperamental inclination in some ways, though historically he thought it marred by a 'stiff legalism' and found the glow of the Enlightenment too thin and too cold. But by the time he was twenty he had taken the high road to England, and by his early thirties was not only marked for life with the stamp of Oxford but called to the English Bar and married into upper-class England. Like many Scots who have taken the same road he could feel and express an aching intensity of love for the sights and sounds of Scotland without any heartbreak at not living there permanently.

Superficially he might seem anglicised: a Scotsman who not only got on but had gone native in Oxford and the West End, at much at home in the Oxfordshire countryside and the Cotswolds as on the Border hills - still Presbyterian but in congregations which the uninstructed English might think of as the Caledonian Society at prayer. Even his voice, to judge from BBC recordings that survive, had lost much of its Scottishness in developing a distinctive character, though some of what seems forced and ornate in it today reflects changes in style and vocal fashions over the last sixty years or so. Any superficial assessment of Buchan's Scottishness based only on his most popular novels might also suggest that by the time of his greatest popularity it had become no more than a veneer. In *The Thirty-nine Steps* and *Mr Standfast*, hurriedly read at a pace to match that of the plots, the Scottish settings may seem no more than a scenic backdrop. Then after the war Scotland seems to shrink to the size of a Highland sporting estate in *John Macnab*, peopled by hearty lairds and their jolly daughters in tweeds, with a few pawky natives to testify to Buchan's memory for the pith and rhythms of Scots vernacular - and with Dickson McCunn at large in Galloway, rich in redeeming features but still a kailyard sort of hero saddled with poorer plots than Richard Hannay would have tolerated. *Witch Wood* was clearly a different matter, but this was a romance without a happy ending and overshadowed by clouds of darkness.

In any event it seemed to relate to distant Scottish history and not to the brave new world of Ramsay MacDonald.

But such judgments are superficial. Buchan's problem was partly that his thrillers were good enough to be taken seriously (as the best of them deserve, provided the confines of the genre are recognised) and popular enough for their memory to become more significant in shaping his posthumous reputation than the serious books which took so much more time and trouble to write and which were extravagantly praised but not nearly so widely read.

The thrillers and romances themselves reflect Buchan's love for Scotland in ways appropriate to the genre and subordinate to the plot. There are dark doings on the Fife shore before *Prester John* moves to testify to Buchan's brief, vivid, and heartfelt encounter with Africa. There is the simple love of the Galloway hills and occasional use of Scots in *The Thirty-nine Steps* and later in the adventures of Dickson McCunn. There is a wider view of Scottish landscape, including the smoke-laden industrial landscape of Clydeside as well as the skirts of the Cuillin, in *Mr Standfast*. There are the salmon-beats and deer-forests of *John Macnab*. Even such a modest book as *The Free Fishers* suddenly comes to life with the sparkle of St Andrews on a clear day and the whiff of fish and the North Sea. On such occasions Buchan's love of the natural landscape of Scotland and the environment and diversity of its people are on a par with the great hymn of praise to Scotland that Eric Linklater put into the mind and mouth of Magnus Merriman.

But a far wider range of Buchan's work - creative, critical, historical, and reflective - needs to be taken into account in assessing his contribution to Scottish culture and his insights into the Scottish identity. There the key texts are his lives of Scott and Montrose and his anthology of Scots poetry, *The Northern Muse*, with a provocative introduction rich in disputable opinions: but by no means always the opinions that might be expected from a Scot who was prospering at the end of the high road to England. He wrote in 1924 when Hugh MacDiarmid (represented in the anthology as C.M. Grieve by *The Bonnie Broukit Bairn*) was beginning to make his impact, and it is arguable whether MacDiarmid's later achievement, and that of Lorimer's New Testament, would have rebutted or reinforced Buchan's conviction that 'Scots can survive only as a book-tongue, and it is to that purpose that I would bespeak the efforts of my countrymen.' Disliking the patois of the towns as bidding fair 'to become merely a broadened and dilapidated English', Buchan expected the Scots to be 'eternally distinguishable' from their southern neighbours, but in voice and accent rather than language. 'To restore the Scots vernacular is beyond the power of any Act of Parliament, because the life on which it depended has gone.'

Fervent cultural patriots who dislike this view may still find it hard to disprove it. It was a subject on which Buchan wrote with passion, authority, erudition, and some very decided opinions. One was his insistence that Burns's poetry did not use the living language of his countrymen but created a literary language of his own as the channel for his genius. Another was his lament for the decay of the Scots he had learned in the Tweedside glens, which 'was then the speech of a people secluded from the modern world'. Yet his emotion made him hard, almost harsh, when assessing the sentimentality of the Kailyard school, 'who harp on obvious pathos till the last trace of pathetic vanishes'. Was it a classical or a Calvinist ideal that subconsciously influenced his austere judgments, even at the expense of such good poets, which he recognised they were, as Hogg and Tannahill?

Yet has any subsequent cultural nationalist matched his assessment that 'Scots poetry is like some cathedral of the Middle Ages, with peasants gossiping in the nave and the devout at prayer in side chapels, carved grotesques adjacent to stained-glass saints, and beams of heavenly light streaking through the brooding upper darkness'?

The irony of this austere and severe passion for Scots culture was that - if Buchan's memory did not play him false - he acquired it at Oxford. Before then, he claimed, he had known relatively little Scottish literature, even Burns; and at Oxford he found time to become a fervent admirer of Burns, as well as Dunbar and the other poets of the Scots tongue's golden age. It was a more lasting influence on him than his revival of the Caledonian Club there, limited to those of proven Scots descent for at least three generations and dining in a green and purple uniform intended to represent the thistle in flower. But he claimed it was part of the same process of acquiring all the characteristics of the Scot abroad.

The area of Scottish literature which he had known from boyhood was the one most closely related to the Border country he loved: the ballads and Sir Walter Scott; and that early affinity with the great Edinburgh Borderer was to mature and influence his own understanding and expression of Scottish identity. Buchan and Scott were both romantics. They were both passionate Scottish patriots - and both anglophiles. They were both Tories, though in the sense of seeking a political affinity for their romanticism rather than being especially reactionary among political conservatives. Both were reinforced in their conservatism by revolutionary tumults in Continental Europe and by the way that war on a new scale seemed to threaten their civilisation. Both worked the Cavalier or Jacobite seam in Scottish history but were passionately devoted to the monarchy as it evolved fom the Whig Revolution settlement. Both were elders of the Kirk, though it was Buchan who lasted that course better.

The parallel should not be taken too far. Buchan was a thinker on matters spiritual and temporal in a way Scott was not and Buchan, as a novelist, never aspired to Scott's achievement or influence. And the one indexed reference to Edinburgh, scene of Scott's triumphs and tragedies, in Buchan's autobiography is about the castle as 'a milestone on the way' from Fife to the Borders. Yet there was enough in common to draw Buchan to Scott, amd to draw out of him the biography which may be his best and even his most important 'serious' book. In writing it he was also drawn into some of his best exploration of Scottish identity.

For Buchan Scott was, with Burns, Scotland's great liberator ond reconciler. 'He seems to me the greatest, because the most representative of Scotsman, since in his mind and character he sums up more fully than any other the idiomatic qualities of his countrymen and translates them into a universal tongue.' Burns had 'burned up much folly with the fires of poetry'; Knox gave Scotland a Reformation which was 'an inestimable but a perilous gift which led to high spiritual exaltations but also to much blood and tears.' Scott was Scotland's Hosea - alluring her, speaking comfortably to her, giving her a door of hope, 'and she shall sing there as in the days of her youth'. (Hosea 2.14-15)

Buchan's own superb prose - as crafted for this high purpose as the terse narratives of Richard Hannay were for the best thrillers - merges into some the noblest eloquence of the Authorised Version. It is rhetorical; but so were the Old Testament prophets. What is easily overlooked, however, is that when he wrote his biography for the centenary of Scott's death he deliberately set it in the context of two trends which have become even more significant in the sixty or so years since. First he knew that Scott was going out of favour - as he recognised at the start of a BBC talk marking the 1932 centenary. Scott's appeal wasn't what it was, he said; the tide of fashion was running away from him. That process has continued. Yet Scott was probably the greatest Scottish influence not only on English literature but on European culture. He continues to inspire good Scottish literature - see for example Allan Massie's 1994 novel about Scott's life, *The Ragged Lion* - but, as Massie testifies in his introduction, still waits in the sure and certain hope of popular rehabilitation. Buchan was a romantic in many ways, as well as a man of faith. Neither his romanticism nor his faith got in the way of his realism about some of the trends, cultural as well as political, which began in his time and have continued into ours.

Secondly, Buchan wrote his biography in the years when political nationalism began to emerge in Scotland both as a significant political force and as a structured one. A Home Rule Bill won substantial support, though it had not got through Parliament. A National Party of Scotland was founded in

1928 and John MacCormick launched a 'Covenant' in 1930 to try to unite different nationalist, home rule, and even revolutionary tendencies in support of a Scottish Parliament. A moderate Scottish Party, including such former Conservatives as Andrew Dewar Gibb, took shape in 1932 and merged in 1934 with the National Party of Scotland (which had shed some extremists) as the Scottish National Party: the S.N.P. of subsequent continuous, if sometimes turbulent, existence. When Buchan wrote his life of Scott at the beginning of the 1930's the political movement might stilll seem a cloud no bigger than a man's hand, but Buchan recognised its potential.

He wrote about Scott as a Scottish nationalist; he professed to be one himself, as indeed the first Labour Premier, Ramsay MacDonald, had done some years earlier. In the House of Commons debate on the address in 1932 Buchan testified to a belief 'that every Scotsman should be a Scottish nationalist', and accepted that a separate Scottish Parliament should be supported if 'proved' desirable. 'I would go further. Even if it were not proved to be desirable, if it could be proved to be desired by any substantial majority of the Scottish people, then Scotland should be allowed to make the experiment...'

Although the practical thrust of the spech was to support the creation of what became St Andrew's House, and the administrative devolution which it fostered, it sympathised with what Buchan thought lay behind the politics of the new nationalism: a belief that Scotland was losing its historic individuality. 'It seems to many that we are in danger of reaching the point when Scotland will have nothing distinctive to show to the world.'

These were close to themes developed in his life of Scott, in which he wrote of the 'the sane and honourable nationalism' of Scott's *Letters of Malachi Malagrowther*, which, although provoked by a proposal to restrict the Scottish banks' issue of notes, reflected wider economic discontents of a Scotland in whose post-Napoleonic-war conditions Buchan probably found some parallels with the troubles of the Great Depression. He enjoyed quoting Scott's famous sentence: 'If you unscotch us you will find us damned mischievous Englishmen.'

By nationalism Buchan did not mean the policy of sovereign independence - first outside the Common Market, then within it - advocated by the modern S.N.P., and he had none of the anglophobia which, although rejected by that party, often seems to mark and even inspire some of those committed to its cause. Those of us who see Scotland rather differently from the S.N.P. would probably draw a distinction between a sense of nationality and 'nationalism'. The distinction is largely the result of subsequent events, for the meaning of words is shaped and sometimes altered by experience. Like many of the moderates in the early S.N.P., Buchan also had a powerful though not a jingoistic commitment to the British Empire. Devotees of Richard Hannay will remember how, under the alias of Twisdon, the trusted leader of Australian thought, he raised a cheer at a Liberal meeting by telling it 'the glorious business I thought could be made out of the Empire if we really put our backs into it'. This is one of the times the voice of Hannay has a ring of Buchan's own views about it. It should also be remembered that during Buchan's political years the hope of Imperial Federation, though fading, was less far-fetched than that of European Union. Had there ever been an imperial Parliament or even standing council of Ministers the question of Scottish devolution would have arisen in a context quite different from that of the second half of the twentieth cenury.

If Buchan had any Scottish nationalist prejudices they were probably inclined against Irish nationalism of the Sinn Fein variety rather than against the English, even in their more expasperating moments. To an extent he did - as some characters in his novels do - reflect the widespread Scottish unease of the time over the consequences of Irish immigration, an anxiety aggravated by ill-feeling over Southern Irish attitudes in the latter part of the war and in the 'Troubles' after it.

When Buchan described the first element in Scott's political faith as 'nationalism' he meant that the great novelist 'believed firmly in the virtues of local patriotism and the idiomatic life of the smaller social unit', and was prepared whenever Scotland was concerned not only to break with his party and his leaders but 'with the whole nobility, gentry, and intellectuality of Britain'.

No more did Buchan use words in the same sense as his political opponents when he claimed that Scott, with his hatred for the rootless and the mechanical, 'had much of that practical socialism which Toryism has never lacked'. Scott certainly had a social conscience that baulked at the calculations of the economists of the day - though he was immensely hostile to incipient trade unionism, was howled down by the Jedburgh weavers for his anti-reform views, and had his carriage stoned on his last election day. Buchan, who was uneasy with the dogmatisms of his own time and a humane pragmatist in his political economics, found in Scott a kindred spirit. For example he shared Scott's inclination 'for the localisation of the issue of credit, which involved the slight inflation that the circumstances of Scotland required, very much in the language of today.'

But it would be pointless to speculate on how Buchan would have related to later trends in Scotland if he had not been diverted in the grand manner to Canada or if he had lived longer. The Scottish Parliament has emerged in a way which seems to vindicate his approach in that 1932 speech on the Address.

His recognition of the importance of Scottish feelings makes him seem wiser than the subsequent leaders of his own political tradition or, for that matter, than the Labour Governments after 1945 and 1964. Too much happened after 1933, however, to justify sweeping assumptions about how Buchan and others would have reacted to later circumstances. For him and for the Scottish people the later 1930's were not primarily a time for introspective reflections on identity and national culture but of increasing anxiety, dread of a new war, and finally acceptance of that ordeal as the lesser evil. The suprising thing is not that much of Buchan's reflection of Scotland's social and cultural condition is time-bound in the late 1920's but that so much has freshness and relevance in a very different Scotland at the turn of the century.

5 CONTINUING RELEVANCE

Fame can fade quickly. Almost all reputations subside in the generation after their subject's death, especially those of eminent persons reckoned to be wise, good, and fashionable: and Buchan had been very fashionable. His autobiography went through 25 reprints in the four years after his death. But wisdom may quickly seem foolishness as conditions change and expectations are unfulfilled. Goodness is often suspect, always probed, sometimes discredited. The greatest danger is to be fashionable for, as fashions change, what had been popular necessarily becomes old-fashioned.

Buchan was inevitably subject to this process, from which many great reputations never recover. Arbiters of literary and social fashion quickly pronounced him old-fashioned, and with him the kind of wisdom and goodness reflected in his work. Richard Hannay was even compared unfavourably with Ian Fleming's tawdry and gaudy creation, James Bond. But Buchan's fall from fame was never as disastrous as might have been feared. More people continued to read his books than heeded the adverse judgments on them - people varying widely in nationality, politics, and religion. Thirty years after his death it was clear that some of his popularity survived; and in the thirty years since then this survival has increasingly become revival.

He is an author who is still enjoyed and appreciated, but he is alao a writer and thinker who deserves to be heeded. There are several important areas, both of literature and life, where he remains relevant and ought to be influential.

The most important of all is his Christian testimony in word and life, along with a demonstration of how the power of intellect and reason can be deployed in a life of faith and, with benefit of grace, even in a culture permeated by non-Christian influences, whether ancient classical or modern agnostic. May there even be more relevance than contemporary Christians realise in the way in which Buchan, like so many others formed by the same culture, incorporated what was best in pre-Christian Hellenism and pagan Rome into their concept of Christian civilisation? They recognised, as we must today in quite different fields, the power of pagan thinking and human reason. But they knew that reason still came third to revelation and redemption.

Buchan writes about the Christian religion with power and authority, uses his understanding of its diversity to deepen his biographies, relates its principles to his politics, and instils its values even into his lighter literature. He also brought its personal values of respect for opponents, even secular dogmatists like some of the early 'Red Clydesiders', into his public and political life. He 'let his moderation be known', both in his parliamentary years and (within severe constitutional limitation) in his term as Governor-General of Canada.

Much of his influence and relevance, however, has a secular application - even if he retained a true Calvinist reluctance to divide human activities neatly into the sacred and the profane.

For example his influence and example should be significant in the literary areas of his greatest success, the thriller and the historical biography. It is possible that his history of the First World War may also become increasingly appreciated. It was written too close to the events to attain historical detachment and without benefit of the vast amount of research which has nourished recent good histories of that war. Yet it contains passages of marvellously sustained eloquence, deep feeling, and great narrative power, as well as reasoned judgments which subsequent research and reflection have not always sustained, but by no means universally contradicted. It has recently been rehabilitated as good history as well as good writing, and future generations may rate it among the significant literature of the 1914-18 war.

In the area of his greatest popularity, Buchan testifies to the way the good thriller depends on good writing and on a story well told and worth telling, as well as on that less definable ability to convey an atmosphere of time, place, and social values. It does not depend for its thrills, like some modern writing, on the grisliness of its violence or the promiscuous acrobatics of its sex. The power of fear and of sex, as well as the dread of violence, are all present in Buchan from time to time: not only in *Witch Wood*, whose theme might be distorted in modern tabloids as 'Kirk elders in witchcraft sex rituals', but in his principal wartime German villains - one by implication homosexual, the other lusting for Mary Lamington, the future Lady Hannay. They also arise in the undescribed dealings of the disguised Sandy Arbuthnot with Hilda von

Einem. Readers may speculate what these involved. But like the best modern thriller-writers - not necessarily Christian or in his literary class - Buchan's success and survival testify an appreciation that for many readers gross sex and violence get in the way of the real thrills of the story.

There is also a lasting significance in Buchan's mastery of historical biography, or the biographical element in history. For history is too important to be left to the professional historians, especially those with no feeling for literature and little contact with public affairs. History is not only about investigating land tenure in Cromwell's youth or the number of daily calories or baggage-waggons required by Covenanting soldiers or Montrose's Highlanders and Irish. It demands an understanding of great passions as well as mixed motives, and not least (in certain ages especially) of passionate religious or ideological convictions and what may seem details of doctrine. It needs not only painstaking concern with factual detail but the imaginative insights into personality which Buchan brought to Montrose and Cromwell and, in a different style and mood, to Sir Walter Scott, whose sense of Scottish identity was so close to his own. His insights into Scott and Montrose, notwithstanding his cavalier treatment of Argyll and Montrose's other Covenanting enemies, are significant contributions to the interpretation of Scottish history, as well as part of Buchan's own expression of Scottish identity.

There are also several aspects of Buchan's expression of Scottish identity, and his reflections on it, which are relevant in the new century to a changing Scotland which sometimes presents itself as a new Scotland.

The first is his sense of the links between Scottish Church and people. This is not a fashionable theme today. Things that he took as self-evident, recognised in his day even by those Scots who did not share his beliefs and traditions, are widely rejected and ignored. But facts are chiels that winna ding. As Buchan wrote in 1930 after the Church reunion: 'Without some understanding of the Church there can be no true understanding of Scottish history or of the nature of the Scottish people.' Scottish society, education, intellect, culture, industry, and science were shaped by the forms the Reformation took in Scotland and the stamp it set on the Scottish people. Those who stand in the tradition of the Reformed faith, with its various strands and imperative for continuing reform, need to understand how the present Church of Scotland came to be; and there is no better guide than Buchan. Other Christians in Scotland, some of them increasingly if unconsciously open to Reformed insights, will find no better interpreter of the Reformed idiom than Buchan, with his broad ecumenical sympathies. Even his argument that Presbyterianism should be a bridge between Nonconformity, in its old religious sense, and Episcopacy can be recast to apply to the new conditions in which great gaps still open up among Christians. And those who reject religion can still neither ignore nor despise it, as the fate of the Soviet empire and Communist ideology has shown.

The second aspect is Buchan's sense of Scottish participation in a much wider world and influence on it. There will always be Scots who shine at Oxford and do well in London; Buchan is a good guide to enjoying that success without losing touch with Scottish roots, although some of his mannerisms and assumptions from Oxford onwards reflect his adjustment to an England more socially stratified then than now. He is also, though one must not stretch arguments in attempts to apply them to quite different political conditions, a good European after his fashion, recognising not only the continental links in Reformed Scottish history but that British involvement in 1914-18 was more than an alliance asserting a balance of power. It was necessary participation, at a fearful cost, in a European civil war. But Buchan will always be a reminder that Scotland looks beyond Europe. His public career began in South Africa and found fulfilment in Canada; and unlike others in the imperial tradition he saw that Britain ought to encourage national reconciliation and national consciousness in both these countries. It is absurd to complain that someone who knew South Africa at the beginning of the century did not see that national consciousness in the terms only generally accepted near the end of it.

His life as well as his thought also testifies to the Scottish role in the British Empire, and his convictions about it reflect the conditions of his time. His son William, the third Lord Tweedsmuir, may have been right to reflect (at the 1991 J.B. Society dinner) that his father was mercifully spared much 'that would have caused him sorrow and exasperation' in the last days of Empire, 'the whole idea of which was so close to his heart'. It is now possible to take a longer view, recognising inevitable trends and avoidable mistakes but appreciating what people like Buchan saw in the imperial idea and contributed to it. But his convictions also recognised that in politics as well as Church affairs reform is a constant process and change an inevitable one.

Buchan's political moderation and sense of Scotland's wider links and distinctive identity also have special relevance to post-imperial Scotland, with its uncertainty over where devolution is to lead. His Scottish patriotism does not provide any formula for the management of a Scottish Parliament or its relationship to Westminster. But it does have lessons for the two main strands in Scottish political thinking, in the broadest sense of that term, in the new century. Those who emphasise the need to assert a Scottish identity, even insist that the logic of devolution must lead to sovereignty, need the humility to recognise that Buchan, like Scott, like countless Scots of lesser distinction, found its possible to sustain, express, and develop a sense of Scottish identity within the Union; and that the triumphs and tragedies of their times (not least the wars) are as much a part Scottish experience and personality as the age of the Makars or the Covenants. Yet those who fear nationalism, or that devolution will breed dissession, must also recognise that a liberal imperialist and Tory moderate of Buchan's calibre was ready to call himself a Scottish nationalist - even if he had not thought of political sovereignty - and to take more satisfaction from Sir Walter Scott's assertion of Scottish rights than his resistance to reform.

Only one thing in Buchan matters more: his conviction that civilisation must have a Christian basis and must ultimately rest not on some vague sense of Judeo-Christian-humanist values but on the Christian Church, fallible though it is as an institution. That is probably a minority view in modern Scotland, and modern Oxford. Both have much in common with the very undevout garden city of Biggleswick in which Richard Hannay nonetheless counted 27 varieties of religious conviction and was warned that 'you will hear everything you regard as sacred laughed at and condemned and every kind of nauseous folly acclaimed'. That Christian conviction, with its balanced view of the Church's authority and the right, even duty, of private judgment, was probably a minority view even when John Buchan expressed it in 1939, but that does not make it wrong.

What he said in 1930 (at the beginning of *The Kirk in Scotland*) of the Church of Scotland surely applies to the whole 'catholick or universal Church', as the Calvinist confession calls it. 'I write as one who believes that the Church throughout its history was divinely inspired, and never in its darkest days ceased to fulfil in some degree its high mission. But I believe, too, that since it was also a human institution officered by fallible men, it blundered often and had many needless years of sojourning in the wilderness. If the spark of celestial origin did not wholly die, other fires burned fiercely which were not divinely kindled. Yet it seems to me that we can discern a real continuity of growth. Slowly, very slowly, it discovered that comprehension was only possible if combined with tolerance.'

Buchan believed passionately in Reformed Christianity and Presbyterian order as a bridge towards wider Christian union. He wanted its example of reform and continuity to link Churches 'rich in historic accretions' with those which expressed movements of the Spirit. Perhaps, if God wills such a bridge to be built and crossed, that quotation from Buchan might be engraved on its stones.

SHORT BIBLIOGRAPHY

A full bibliography for John Buchan would need another booklet. The 'selected list' of his works at the end of John Lownie's biography runs to more than five pages. Lownie's book also includes a very extensive and valuable, yet not exhaustive, list of sources, books, and articles about Buchan or relevant to his work. The John Buchan Society has also gathered a vast amount of bibliographical information. This note includes only what may be regarded as the kernel of a Buchan bibliography.

There are three principal published accounts of his life - his own book-length extended autobiographical essay *Memory Hold-the-Door* (Hodder and Stoughton, 1940) and the biographies by Janet Adam Smith *John Buchan* (Hart-Davis, 1965) and John Lownie, *John Buchan: the Presbyterian Cavalier* (Constable, 1995). Janet Adam Smith had also a shorter book *John Buchan and His World* (Thames and Hudson, 1979), perhaps the most vivid personal portrait.

There is *A Buchan Companion* by Paul Webb (Alan Sutton, 1994). This is a patchy and selective mini-encyclopaedia on Buchan themes and characters, There is also an anthology prepared by Buchan's widow, Susan Tweedsmuir, *The Clearing House* (Hodder and Stoughton, 1946) - important because it reflects what seemed most important to his family in the immediate aftermath of his death, presumably reflecting Buchan's own judgments, for example in a number of passages from his history of the First World War and extracts from lesser-known works.

The fullest 'encyclopaedia', however, is *The John Buchan Journal*, published by the John Buchan Society. It is rich in specialised information as well as devoted enthusiasm. At the time of writing 21 issues have appeared since the first in 1980. The society's secretary is listed in the latest as Kenneth Hillier, Greenmantle, Ingles Hill, Ashby-de-la-Zouche LE65 2TF.

There is a good collection of Buchan memorabilia and photographs in the John Buchan Centre at Broughton, an unpretentious but valuable literary museum. It is in the former Free Church building (which has a Hannay family window!) at the Tweedsmuir end of the village.

Many of Buchan's novels are in print, though booksellers seem uncertain whether to stock them under 'classics', 'Scottish', or general paperback thrillers and fiction. The Nelson reprints are also frequently encountered. Andrew Lownie has collected the short stories in three volumes (Thistle Publishing, 1997) and, with William Milne as co-editor, the poems (Scottish Cultural Press, 1996).

The most important biographies by Buchan, reflecting much of his own thinking, are *Montrose* (Nelson, 1928); *Sir Walter Scott* (Cassell, 1932); and *Oliver Cromwell* (Hodder & Stoughton 1934, more often met with in the 1941 Reprint Society edition).

Buchan and Sir George Adam Smith wrote *The Kirk in Scotland 1560-1929* (Hodder & Stoughton, 1930) to mark the reunion of the Church of Scotland the previous year. Smith provided nearly 100 pages on the reunion General Assemblies, Buchan an essay of 110 pages on the historical background to the union and a 30-page reflection on the future. The original book is now scarce, but a reprint of the Buchan contributions under the 1930 title, with a postscript by me on subsequent Church history, appeared in 1985 (Labarum Press, Dunbar) but without the eminently desirable introduction to establish the context in which Buchan wrote.

The forthcoming *New Dictionary of National Biography* will be valuable, not least because it plans to include notes of film and radio archival material. When I wrote the script for a Radio 4 broadcast on 'The Presbyterian Cavalier' in 1992, with book extracts rendered marvellously by Tom Fleming, the BBC were able to let me hear a 1932 broadcast talk in which Buchan marked the centenary of the death of Sir Walter Scott. Andrew Lownie lists the BBC Records at Caversham but does not say what is available in print, on tape, or both.

ACKNOWLEDGMENTS

I owe much to books about Buchan, notably the biographies by Janet Adam Smith, who died while this book was being set, and Andrew Lownie, as well as to the John Buchan Society and its journal, and to the John Buchan Centre at Broughton. See the short bibliography. The main source for evaluation of Buchan as writer and thinker, however, must be his own books, even though I have not tried to quote or even mention all of them. I record my vast debt to them.

I add my thanks to the Very Revd John McIndoe and the Revd Sandy Cairns of Buchan's London kirk, St Columba's Pont Street, for their help in establishing some important points of detail.

R.D. Kernohan